Team, Yes!

by Phillip Trong • illustrated by Jill Banashek

Orlando   Boston   Dallas   Chicago   San Diego

Visit *The Learning Site!*
www.harcourtschool.com

Teammates are people who work or play together. A team can have many people, or just a few. Two people can be a team. Teams compete with one another. Teams use teamwork to help them win.

A Tennis Team

People usually think of tennis as an individual sport. One player will play against another player. Tennis can be a team sport, too.

Two people on one team can play against two people on another team. In tennis, this is called doubles. Together, the tennis team works to hit the ball over the net to the other team. The team that hits the ball wants the other team to miss the ball.

The other team tries to hit the ball back over the net. The teammates continue hitting the ball over the net to each other until one team misses.

An Ice Skating Team

Like tennis, ice skating can be an individual sport. One skater can compete against other skaters. Each skater receives a score. The skater with the highest score wins the contest.

Skaters who skate in pairs are a team. The team practices long and hard. The team practices new and difficult moves. They must work together. They must help each other, and they must not fall. The skaters depend on each other.

The skating pairs are teammates. They skate together in competitions. Each skating team tries to get points for their routine. The team with the highest score wins.

A Running Team

Running can be an individual sport. One runner can compete against many other runners.

Runners in a relay race are a team. The runners on that team are teammates. Each team has four runners. One runner carries a thin stick called a baton. The runner runs part of the way around a track and gives the baton to the next runner on the team.

The next runner takes the baton and runs part of the way around the track. The runners on a team must work together to pass the baton. They don't want to miss a step!

The strongest runner is the last teammate to run. The last runner on the relay team goes across the finish line. But the whole team wins. The winning team has worked together.

A Gymnastics Team

Gymnastics can be a team sport. Gymnasts compete against other gymnasts. Female gymnasts compete in several events. The events include the balance beam, the vault, and the uneven parallel bars. Male gymnasts have different events. These events include the even parallel bars, the rings, and the pommel horse.

Gymnasts practice together. They help each other, and they give each other ideas on how to do better.

During a competition, each gymnast receives a score. The total scores for all the gymnasts on a team are added together. The team with the highest score wins.

A Basketball Team

Basketball is a team sport. The players on a basketball team are teammates. Two teams of players compete against each other.

Five players from each team are on the basketball court at one time. Each team tries to score as many points as possible. Players score points by throwing a basketball through a net. The net is also called a hoop or a basket.

The net is set high above the players' heads. One net is on each end of a basketball court.

It's not easy to get the ball through the hoop. The players on the other team will put their hands up in the air to stop the ball. They will try to take the ball away. They want to score as many points as possible. It takes teamwork to get the ball into the basket.

   Great teamwork is needed to play basketball. Teammates work together to score points. They work together in different ways. Let's look at two teams: the Blue Team and the Green Team.
   As one player on the Blue Team moves the ball down the court, the other players on the Blue Team get into their places. They pass the ball around to each other. They look for a clear shot to the basket.
   One player on the Blue Team tries to put the ball through the hoop. Players on the Green Team try to stop the ball. The Blue Team tries to stop, or block, the Green Team's players, too.
   The player with the basketball takes aim. The player with the basketball throws the ball. She does it! She scores two points for her team!

A Hockey Team

Instead of running on a wood floor like basketball teams do, hockey teams skate on ice. Instead of shooting baskets, hockey players shoot goals. Instead of passing a basketball back and forth, the players pass a hockey puck back and forth.

In hockey, two teams compete against each other. Players from each team use teamwork to try to score goals. A goal is scored when a member of one team hits the puck into the net of the other team. Just like basketball, one net is on each end of the skating rink.

Players on a hockey team have special equipment. They wear helmets to keep their heads safe. They wear ice skates to get across the rink. They use special sticks to move the hockey puck across the ice. The player at each net wears a face mask.

In hockey, one teammate guards the net. This player is called the goalie. The players on the other team try to get the hockey puck into the net. The goalie's teammates try to keep the hockey puck as far away from their goalie as possible.

It's not always easy! The ice helps the puck move fast. The players move fast, too. They skate from one end of the rink to the other. Both teams chase the puck. Each team tries to take the puck away from the other team.

One player moves the puck with the stick. He passes it to a teammate. This player takes aim and hits the puck. The puck goes into the net! With his teammate's help, the hockey player has made a goal!

A Soccer Team

Soccer is like hockey. Both hockey players and soccer players try to score a goal in the other team's net. Instead of playing on ice, soccer teams play on a grassy field. Instead of passing a hockey puck back and forth, soccer players pass a soccer ball back and forth.

Nets are at each end of the soccer field. Each time a player kicks the ball into the other team's net it is a goal. One goal gets one point for the team. The team with the most points at the end of the game is the winning team.

Players on a soccer team don't need a lot of special equipment. They wear loose shorts and shirts so they can move quickly. Soccer players also wear special shoes called cleats. Cleats help keep soccer players from slipping.

In soccer, one teammate guards the net. This teammate is called the goalie. The teammates on the other team try to kick the soccer ball into the other team's net. The goalie's teammates try to keep the soccer ball as far away from their goalie as possible. Teams use teamwork to make sure the ball stays far away from their goalie.

Only the goalie can use his or her hands to stop or move the ball. The other players are allowed to kick the ball. They are allowed to hit the ball with their heads. They cannot use their hands to pass and move the soccer ball down the field.

The teammates work together to score points. Teammates move the ball toward the net. They pass the ball back and forth. One player takes a shot. She does it! She scores a goal!

A Football Team

During a football game, two teams compete on a grassy field. Instead of trying to score a goal, the players try to score a touchdown. The players throw the football or run with it.

In football, each team tries to score as many points as possible. Players can score points in different ways. A touchdown gets six points. The kick after a touchdown gets one point, and a field goal is three points.

Players on a football team need special equipment. They wear helmets to keep their heads safe. They wear pads to keep their bodies safe. They wear special cleats, too. The shoes help them run on the grass without slipping.

Each football team puts eleven players on the field. The teams take turns playing offense and defense. The quarterback is the leader of the offense team. The quarterback throws the football to a teammate. This teammate is called the receiver. The receiver runs toward the end zone. A touchdown is made when a player takes the ball across the other team's end zone.

The players on defense try to stop the player with the ball. They chase the player across the field. They stop the player by tackling. This means that they try to make the player fall down.

Making a touchdown is very difficult. Winning a football game takes a lot of teamwork!

A Baseball Team

Baseball is a game of hits and runs. Nine players from each team play at one time. All nine players on the team get turns at bat. This means that they each get a chance to hit the baseball. The goal is to hit the ball and reach a base safely.

A baseball diamond has four bases: first base, second base, third base, and home plate. The batters start at home plate. This is where they try to hit the ball. When they do hit a ball, they must try to reach a base before a player on the other team tags them out. When they cross home plate again, they score one run. The team that scores the most runs wins the game.

When a team is not at bat, the players are out in the field. They try to stop the other team from getting to a base. They also try to stop the other team's players from getting to home plate.

Each player in the field has a job. The pitcher throws the ball for the batter to hit. The catcher catches the ball when the batter cannot hit it. The catcher throws the ball back to the pitcher to throw again.

Four players work together around the bases. These players are called infielders. Infielders guard first base, second base, and third base. One player guards the space between second and third base. This player is called the *shortstop.*

Three players work together outside the bases. These players are called outfielders. Players in the outfield work together to catch balls hit by the other team. They try not to let the other team score runs.

    You don't have to play a sport to be part of a team. Your class is a team. Your classmates are teammates. Your family is a team. Your family members are teammates. You work with your classmates and family members to solve problems and to help one another. So whether you are playing a sport or working on a project, teamwork is important.

    Working with a team is fun. Each team member is important to the team. Players on a team know they must help one another win.